To Flee the Snare

Kit Karpiak

BookLeaf
Publishing

India | USA | UK

Presentation by *BookLeaf Publishing*

Web: www.bookleafpub.com

E-mail: info@bookleafpub.com

ISBN: 9789360946951

First edition 2024

For everyone.

breath

you find yourself alone after a blizzard
the chill like a live wire under your skin
and a silence so heavy that it pulls your body
downwards, towards the unmarked snow
it's the kind of quiet that you can feel
like standing at the top of an old staircase
which leads deep into the ancient cellar
of a house that was once a home
but has since been reclaimed by nature

you find yourself alone after a blizzard
your forest, an alien landscape transformed
your trees, your ferns, your paths no more
sleeping beneath so much snow
and there isn't a soul around for guidance
to tell you where you came from
or where you might find yourself
there is nothing but the snow
and the slumbering trees
you hold your breath
silence

you find yourself alone after a blizzard
excitement, like the chill under your skin
you take the first step
and leave an imprint in the snow

color

and should he ever turn,
to face the vibrant sky
its bright colors would burn

into his dull gray eye
the sun, a searing brand
of what he can't espy

against his nerves like sand
but through the twisting pain
he reaches out a hand

to touch the window pane
and feel the warmth therein
when colors, boundless, stain

their mark upon his skin
and shocked, he looks to see
a light blooming within

himself; what he can be
that he can touch the light
with no more agony

his own reflection bright,

so deeper out he delves
yes, we are the sunlight;

and we create ourselves.

small, soft thing

when a snowdrop first peeks above the frost
tiny soft petals touch the bracing cold
and in that frozen place, defy the winter's chill
like how the striking of an old lighter
will inspire a fragile yellow flame
to challenge the infinite dark

what refute has the dark?
likewise, what says the frost?
when this minuscule flower dispels it like flame
too dispels the darkness, and scares away the
cold
and yet unlike its brother, the lighter
whose blossoming flames know only how to
combat the chill

this flower, impossibly small, is welcomed by
the chill
who after an eternity of dark
yearns even for the burn from a lighter
if only to end the unfeeling frost
and breach the stoic cold
which would give anything to touch the flame

but this is not a flame
it does not smite the chill
it will not end the cold

it does not fear the dark
it coexists with frost
it will never be a lighter

and so, drawn to its warmth, unlike burning
from a lighter
the winter tends the snowdrop as a human tends
a flame
it watches the flower embrace the frost
and with joy, swaddles it in chill
protects it from the dark
and grows it in the cold

in nurturing this small creature, the cold
forgets its fear of the lighter
and learns to love the dark
laughs mirthfully in the face of the flame
because nothing can stop its chill
from nurturing this small, soft thing which loves
the frost

until the cold
forgets the flame

and spring, like a lighter
leaves naught but the memory of a chill

reserved for the coldest dark
when the small, soft thing remembers the frost

it should

does the bug marvel
at the smell of leaves beneath
its feet when it rains

bloom

when winter ends and the world is again teeming
with life
flowers of every color splash the countryside in
vivid hues
and everything is golden and alive
it's a color that you can taste
a warmth that you can feel in the back of your
throat
heavy, nearly suffocating
but you drink it in, because it tastes like the earth
smells
after its first rain
the bright yellow of daffodils against crystalline
white snow
buttercups dotting a meadow like so many
fragrant stars

when was the first time that you truly noticed
spring?
the distinction between winter's sterile cold,
and the cacophony of sickly sweet smells and
lights
dizzying in their excitement
mine was at an amusement park
rain still hung in the air
birds sang over the whirring of roller coasters
you took my hand, and I bloomed

guts

they reach inside of my small intestine
and drag the outsides in
what they see delights and disgusts
they giggle, prod, and sin
as for me, I mustn't react
must let them follow their whim
as man and woman alike decree
that they know best what's within

and once their cannibal feast is through
their needles pierce my skin
I speak with them as they drain my blood
gawk at the phials and grin
for what am I if not a creature
an oddity, a scientific win
at least once all is said and done, they'll deign
to let me be myself again

bigdog

soft
shadows like fur
big, cool tufts
a photo negative
the light ebbs
he grows
and I am safe

nightblind

and she sees it
that one golden thing
encased in fire as
the sun burns
forever taunting freezing fingertips

it feels like dying
when she plunges her hand into the flame

she holds on

never found

says the fox to her trembling kits:
see that you're never found
the bear will beg your audience
then feed you to the ground

do not heed the lies that stain
deep red his jagged teeth
lest you will soon join them
and learn of what's beneath

in this world of animals
the trees sing our names
just that those who hunt us
will bring them down in flames

but mother, mewls a kit
what life is that to lead?
a lifetime spent in darkness
no sunlight for the seed

should we keep to the shadows
and keep mum our own name
what good is a forest
that lives in fear of flame?

if every waking moment
is spent hiding from the bear
what proof have we, when life is done
that we were ever there?

a chill sweeps through the forest
the fox curls around her kits
then speaks, after some respite
sharp pupils changed to slits:

oh my sweet soft youngling,
her dark voice sounds amused:
we don't hide from the bear
that's the beauty of the ruse:

we are never found.

something new

when it peels apart its chrysalis
does it think it's been reborn
did it know that it was merely sleeping
or did it struggle against the
inexplicable urge to suffocate itself
as thread oozed from its thorax
and coated its soft body
until it was buried in a silken tomb

did it mourn, when it lost the fight?
did it assume that all was lost?
did it give up, and spend days waiting
for the moment that it would stop breathing
only to learn of no such respite

when did it start to fight back?
how many hours were spent in darkness
before arms burst from its ribs
and pounded at the confines
of its hardened chrysalis;
the tomb created by its own body

and what of when it breached the shell
many hands reaching outward
palms upturned in reverence

to again touch the air?

did it shake its trembling wings
and feel the cool air on their scales?
taste the cool night air
with different lips, which found it sweeter?
and then, with a joy unlike anything
that it had ever tasted
did it spread its newborn wings
and know intuitively
that it could fly?
or did it merely

jump

rain

that space between spring
and winter, when the raindrops
contain city lights

冬と春
に間の場,雨は
光を持つ

corpseflower

sometimes spring devours winter
flowers feast on rotting flesh
dirt peeks through snow as bruises
bloom beneath festering maggots
who feast on refuse to birth flowers
that eat their surroundings to make spring

sometimes death masquerades as spring
because flora and fauna who thrive in winter
find their corpses food for flowers
who care not if their prosperity is born of
suffering flesh
this kind of spring has no love for the maggots
who toil away to create it by burrowing into soft
bruises

sometimes spring is bruises
it is watching with dread as winter turns to
spring
it is an uncaring god taking delight in maggots
in the plague that he released to end his winter
by loosing them into your flesh
to make tunnels for so many thorned flowers

sometimes a place isn't meant to have flowers

if their presence demands bruises
and peels away the soft flesh
all for nothing but to delight a spring
which lives only to dominate winter
by burying it in maggots

and then telling it to love the maggots
because they make way for flowers
sometimes winter is just winter
it does not want its snow to give way to bruises
it has no interest in melting for spring
or watching a twisted god devour flesh

sometimes things which devour flesh
are no better than the writhing maggots
which they employ to commence "spring"
winter can grow its own flowers
snowdrops, daffodils, crocuses; all of which do
not need bruises
and do not compete with winter

a spring that demands flesh
in order to grow its flowers

will never exceed the maggots
and its hunger for bruises

if such a thing can truly be called spring,
I'd rather winter.

the man at the end of the
street

imagine walking in a dream
body heavy, full of sand that
forms a dark river, dragging you
down, into the inky escape

you're outside, rain is pouring from
a pitch black sky and onto him

Autumn Leaves

Life is short
Summer's sweet
Let's waste time in the
Autumn leaves

I'll only be around for
Just a little while
So let's waste the day
Making each other smile

This life is short
But autumn is sweet
So I'll spend my time
With the autumn leaves

It isn't winter yet.

autumn leaves (reprise)

Winter came to kill the leaves
Snow laid claim to hills and eaves
Cold did maim the ill naives
Together, we endured it

You and I survived the cold
True that I strived to unfold
The do or die contrived to hold
Us down until we would quit

Out of winter so came spring
Devout through splintered suffering
We shout to inter winter's sting
Though it can't harm us one bit

Watch us laugh and dance and thrive
We'd half a chance to be alive
Through staff and lance we did arrive
So light, we choose to emit

And now life is a merry skit
Past ire and strife as fairies flit
Don't tire o'er trifling scary shit
Because we know that we'll survive

Through thick and thin we will stay fit
We're quick and nimble, won't submit
To tricky nits' chagrin we quit
Their game of painful waiting

I know it's rude to brag, innit?
But dude we got that bag, a crit
Nat 20, crude? Too bad, my writ
frees me from doing as I'm told

This poem thaws the skin un-slit
Opponens Pollicis re-knit
Cause in the end, winter I split
And bid adieu the autumn leaves

larvae

larvae who witness butterflies
assume that they are fairies
they live in fear of magic
so they trundle far away
from the vibrant colors
and flapping wings
to scorn those who
would touch the heavens
with velveteen antennae

these larvae fight with iron wills
to never metamorphose
as their thoraxes spin fresh silk
sharp jaws descend to taper
soft flesh until nothing is left
but gooey insides
and the fear of becoming colorful

the last firefly

imagine the vacant expanse of a grassy field
beneath an endless swathe of spattered stars
a single yellow light blips into existence
amidst the cacophony of singing crickets

does it look up at the stars
and through compound eyes
mistake their light for kindred spirits?

from the grave

pull me from the grave
show me that you're not afraid
like the scalpel to my brain
shock my senses, break the chains
I need your blood in my veins
animating my remains
I'm a zombie, you're a flame
burn my body, scream my name

push me back into the ground
tear my stitches, flesh unbound
liberating what you found
rip my heart out, make it pound
break my silence with your sound
breathless lungs another round
blue lips breathe but to expound
reverence, your name renowned

gemini

as the moon wanes
it will wax again.
is it not the moon
without the sun?

only the dead cast no shadows

there is beauty in a flickering floodlight
in the inky blackness at the end of a forested
path
in the dull glow of an ancient greenhouse
against the infinite backdrop of nothing

there is beauty in the cool embrace of a shadow;
in the way that it clings to your skin,
and makes the street lights seem
ever brighter

To Flee The Snare

Beneath the ocean cave
Lungs are full of water
A cold and biting grave

Air rises when it's hotter
So too goes my body
Lamb unto the slaughter

My refuge dank and shoddy
I rise again alone
No sign of anybody

With air I'm on my own
Without food I will die
The water's lapping drone

Entices me to try
Again into its depth
I dive to breathe, to cry

Though I know not its breadth
(The cold, unfeeling sea)
I hold my straining breath

Claw deeper, to be free

For at this tunnel's end
I must believe there'll be

The respite of a friend
Or sunlight's warming rays
I swim around the bend

But it goes on a ways
And I am out of air
But I will not retrace

The steps which got me there
I live to see the sun
I die to flee the snare

www.ingramcontent.com/pod-product-compliance
Lightning Source LLC
La Vergne TN
LVHW021344200726
843509LV00014B/2664